CW00832189

# FAMIL

## IN THE

# STAFFORDSHIRE PEAK

# & POTTERIES

## Les Lumsdon

Maps by Pam Upchurch

Scarthin Books, Cromford, Derbyshire    1990

# FAMILY WALKS
# IN THE STAFFORDSHIRE PEAK & POTTERIES

*Family Walks Series*
General Editor: Norman Taylor

---

## THE COUNTRY CODE
Guard against all risk of fire
Fasten all gates
Keep dogs under proper control
Keep to paths across farm land
Avoid damaging fences, hedges and walls
Leave no litter
Safeguard water supplies
Protect wildlife, wild plants and trees
Go carefully along country roads
Respect the life of the countryside

---

Published 1990

Phototypesetting, printing by Higham Press Ltd., Shirland, Derbyshire

*ISBN 0 907758 34 7*

BUTTERTON

## Dedication

To Alex, Gina and Leila

---

## The Author

Les Lumsdon has written several previous books about walking including *Staffordshire Walks . . . Simply Superb, Shropshire Walks, Twenty Great Walks from British Rail* and *Great Walks from Welsh Railways,* the latter two with co-author Colin Speakman. He has also written a number of booklets with Martin Smith including *Buxton Spa Line . . . Rail Rambles* and *Rail Rambles in The Hope Valley.* The titles reflect his interest in leaving the car behind whenever possible. Les lives at Macclesfield in Cheshire and is married with three children. He is a Senior Lecturer in Tourism at Staffordshire Polytechnic.

---

## Acknowledgement

Thanks to Angie Rann, Tourism Officer, Staffordshire Moorlands.

# CONTENTS

# MAP OF THE AREA

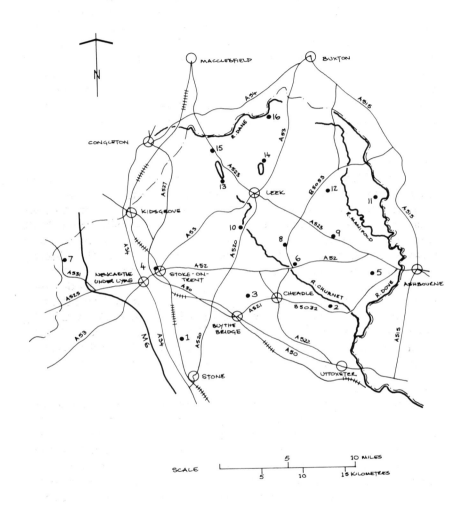

SCALE

# Introduction

Counting the number of steps down the Devil's Staircase, exploring the lost river of the Manifold and scrambling the rocky Roaches are just some of the things children love to do on rambles in North Staffordshire. It is without doubt a place for family walking. The variety of scenery within such short distances is unbeatable. Many of the paths are far less busy than elsewhere even on Sunday afternoons. The same applies to the village and country inns en route. What's more, this area spanning the Southern Peak District and the Staffordshire Moorlands, offers such an interesting range of attractions from narrow boat trips to one of the most exciting theme parks in Europe, Alton Towers.

## Varied Scenery

North Staffordshire's landscape is partly dominated by moorlands broken only by rocky outcrops and streams plunging down cloughs. A few miles north of Leek in the heart of the Staffordshire Moorlands, lies the most impressive of these edges - The Roaches. The name derives from the French 'Roche' meaning rock and the weird shapes of these windswept rocks with equally imaginative names such as The Winking Man, Hen Cloud, Witherspool is a fascination to young and old alike. To the west, in the Southern Peak District, the terrain is gentler with undulating pastureland dissected by miles of drystone walls which shine almost white in the sun. This area known as the 'White Peak', lying in the southernmost part of the Peak National Park, offers a number of walks which dip into the steeply sided dales, beautiful valleys often bereft of water and hence the subject of great family discussion.

## Visitor Attractions

There is another part of North Staffordshire, a part not so well known but nevertheless equally engaging. Perhaps, it is because The Potteries is so renowned as a china manufacturing area that we tend to forget all the other attractions. With world famous names such as Royal Doulton, Wedgwood, Minton and Spode it is not surprising. Needless to say, there are stretches of beautiful countryside within easy reach of the six, (not five as Arnold Bennett has written) pottery towns. This adds to the overall appeal. Even when there is only a day to spare, the morning can be devoted to a factory tour, observing at first hand the delightful process of making fine bone china out of clay. The afternoon is then free to walk in and around nearby villages, not changed much over the centuries, even though an industrial revolution has taken place almost around the corner!

## About the walks

The walks vary from 1½ to 6½ miles and are shown in order of difficulty in the Appendices. Most of the walks have escape routes. All of the family might be keen when they set off but if, after the first mile or so, the mood changes then all is not lost by a shorter return to the starting point. For many, the suggested routes need be for guidance only. A visit to Cheddleton, for example, would still bring an opportunity to walk along the Caldon Canal and without undertaking the longer ramble outlined in the book.

With the exception of the canalside walk in Stoke-on-Trent all others are unsuitable for 'buggies' and even the towpaths are uneven. Most of the walks, however, are achievable for those with little legs. It is very often a question of pace, picnic and pastimes. Each walk includes possible questions or puzzles to keep the team thinking while on the move.

## Clothing

The walks have all been researched during one of the driest years for a long time. Needless to say, whatever the season, make sure you have protective clothing to keep out the wet in case the weather turns against you. As important is to wear stout footwear. Children resist walking boots so in dry weather go for 'trainers'. If it is wet though, wellies with a good grip will save wet feet. It goes without saying that the entire family needs proper outdoor clothing if venturing out in the colder months. While the walks are short and mainly in gentler terrain, a nasty storm can be frightening if you are not wrapped up appropriately.

## The Paths

After rain, paths can get muddy. After all, it is a working countryside and cows and sheep tend to churn up tracks and field corners. Expect to come across wet sections. It is also important to realise that on some of the walks you will pass herds of cattle grazing, and on others crops growing. All of the walks follow rights of way and this means that the path should not be obstructed by a crop, a barbed wire fence or anything else for that matter. Most people go for a common sense approach of choosing the nearest easy way around such a blockage and report it to the County Council Footpaths Officer afterwards.

Stiles come in all shapes and sizes and children love them. The instructions are written as if your back is to the stile and with the accompanying map should be sufficient for successful navigating. However, if you like maps you will need the Ordnance Survey Landranger sheets 118 and 119. Some people prefer the Pathfinder sheets which detail most paths in a given locality and several are on sale in all of the local Tourist Information offices and bookshops. The Outdoor Leisure Map No. 24, The Peak District - White Peak, is very useful.

## Timing

Walks with children are difficult to time. Allow a fair amount of time for fun, exploration and the all important picnic or pub stop. As a rough yardstick a young child will need about an hour for one mile, a ten year old will be sprinting along at well over 2 miles per hour.

## Refreshments

A stop at a local inn en route can improve the walk considerably! Publicans generally welcome families at lunchtimes and at early evening. Virtually all places mentioned in this book have a garden or outdoor area suitable for families, some with swings and slides. Most provide food. In fact, many depend on it for their living so they do not take kindly to customers eating their own sandwiches!

North Staffordshire has a large number of country pubs and unlike other parts of the country they are not packed to the point where they become uncomfortable. There are, unfortunately, fewer surviving village stores and post offices. They can often provide cartons of drinks and the naughty nibble for the latter part of the walk.

## Public Transport

Wherever feasible, public transport access has been included. Cars, as we all know well have their disadvantages environmentally and not everyone has access to one at any given time. Bearing these points in mind many of the walks are achievable by bus or train without any real difficulty. Even if you are tempted to take the car, why not try out the train to Wedgwood or Barlaston or 'The Moorland Rider' on summer Sundays out from Newcastle-under-Lyme and Leek into the Staffordshire Moorlands. Using the bus or train, even for short distances, is a fascination to younger children. The easiest way to obtain up to date information is to 'phone Staffordshire Busline on (0785) 223344.

The family will also welcome the opportunity to try out the Foxfield and North Staffordshire Steam Railways in addition to the miniature gauge Lakeside Railway at Rudyard. These operate usually at weekends (with steam mainly on Sundays) during the main season but the Santa Claus specials at the North Staffs Railway during December also attract a good number. A walk to see Santa and a short steam train ride works wonders.

# Symbols used on the route maps

| | |
|---|---|
| — — —▶— — — — | Route |
| — · — ·>· — · — | Alternative Route |
| ~~~~~~~~~~ | Road or Track |
| — — — — — — — — | Footpath **not** on route |
| ～～～～ | River |
| ⊥⊥⊥⊥⊥⊥ | Canal |
| ┼┼┼┼┼┼┼──── | Railway |
| + | Church |
| ▪ ▪ | Buildings |
| ♀ ♀ ♀ | Woodland |
| ③ | Number (3 etc.) corresponds with route description |

# Route 1

## Barlaston and Wedgwood

**Outline**   Barlaston  ∼  Trent  and  Mersey  Canal  ∼  Wedgwood  ∼ Barlaston.

**Summary**   This gentle walk across fields to the Trent and Mersey Canal and then along the towpath to Wedgwood is a good starter ramble for younger members of the family especially as there is a cut-off point at Barlaston Railway Station and at Wedgwood too if a train to Barlaston is due. The paths are well walked and easy to follow but take care when crossing the tracks at Wedgwood.

**Attractions**   Barlaston village green is a tidy looking place and a sharp glance at the bye laws will explain why ... "A person shall not, on any part of the village green, beat, strike, sweep, brush, or cleanse any carpet, drugget, rug or hat or any fabric retaining dust or dirt." A fine of forty shillings for such misdemeanours does seem a bit lenient but the bye laws do date from 1910!

Opposite is the old school, dating from the 18th century and now a library.

The major attraction of the area is the Wedgwood factory. This internationally recognised pottery manufacturer attracts visitors from all over the world to see the making of fine bone china at the Visitor Centre, now open seven days a week. Wedgwood was, by all accounts, a remarkable man, not only as a potter but also as a scientist and humanitarian. Born in Burslem in 1730, the youngest of twelve, he served several apprenticeships before establishing his own works in Burslem. The business flourished thanks to Wedgwood's keen sense of direction and commercial flair. The present factory in Barlaston replaced the Etruria works just after the Second World War.

Barlaston Hall and Church can be seen from your walk across parkland on the return stretch to Barlaston. This was built for a Mr. Thomas Mills, a wealthy attorney from Leek, and while it has been in decay for decades, restoration of the building has taken place recently. The church contains many monuments to the Wedgwood family.

Besides train spotting and counting the boats along the Trent and Mersey Canal the children might also imagine what it would have been like building these major waterways two hundred years ago. What would the life of the navvy have been like?

*continued on page 11*

9

# Route 1

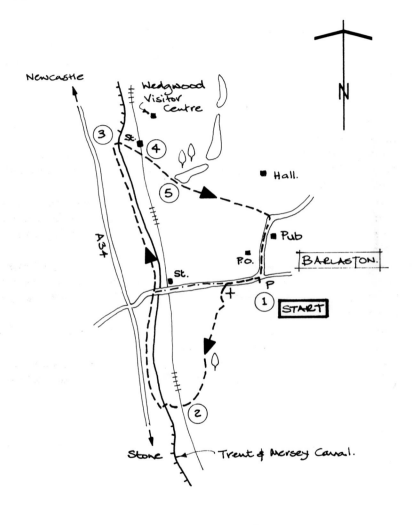

Newcastle

Wedgwood Visitor Centre

③

St.

④

⑤

Hall.

A34

Pub

P.O.

BARLASTON.

St.

P

+

① START

②

Stone

Trent & Mersey Canal.

N

SCALE : 1 MILE (1.6 km)

# Route 1

## Barlaston and Wedgwood                    **3 miles**

START  *From the car park at Barlaston Green (O.S. Sheet 127 G.R.
894384). Barlaston is signed off the main A34 road between Newcastle
and Stone. Rail travellers may join the route at Wedgwood or Barlaston
Railway Stations.*

ROUTE

1. *From Barlaston Car Park turn left and left again alongside the main
   road. After the church turn left over a stile and follow the track to
   another stile. Cross it and go right. This leads to a copse in the corner of
   the field. Cross the stile here, and go left, following the field's edge, until
   it nears the railway, where you cross the stile on your left.*
2. *Turn right and go under the railway, then go over the canal bridge. Go
   down to the left to reach the towpath, then turn left to follow the towpath
   alongside the Trent and Mersey Canal through Barlaston village and on
   to Wedgwood.*
3. *Your exit is Bridge Number 104, where you see the Wedgwood factory
   to your right. On the road go right for a few steps, then go right again to
   cross a stile. The well worn path leads to the railway, which must be
   crossed with great care.*
4. *Follow the path ahead to the right of the wood, cross a stile and walk the
   short stretch to the green gate at the head of a pond.*
5. *Go through a kissing gate and follow the well defined path to Barlaston
   village. Turn right and walk along the roadside path by the pub and post
   office to the village green.*

ACCESS BY BUS AND TRAIN
Barlaston is served by P.M.T. bus 47 and by train, as is Wedgwood on
   Mons.-Sats.

————————

**Refreshments**
   There is a public house by the canal at Barlaston and also one in the
village near the green.

LOCK-UP AT ALTON

# Route 2
**3 miles**

## Alton

**Outline**   Alton ~ Saltersford Lane ~ Churnet Valley ~ Alton.

**Summary**   Alton is a fine looking village, nestled on the edge of the deeply incised Churnet Valley and distinguished by a mock Gothic castle perched on a craggy precipice. It is hardly surprising that earlier writers have nick-named this part of the Churnet 'Staffordshire's Little Rhineland'. This walk allows you to leave behind the busier paths towards Dimmingsdale and Ousal Dale, although very pleasant they are. It also allows a break from the non stop traffic flow on its way to nearby Alton Towers. The walk joins the Staffordshire Way, an excellent long distance path, traversing the entire county from Mow Cop in the North to Kinver in the deep South. It then drops quite steeply into the Churnet and returns by way of the trackbed of the old Churnet Valley railway line, finally to climb back up into the village. The views are exquisite.

**Attractions**   The countryside in this area is rather romantic, a blend of woodland, pastures and traditional Moorland farmland broken up by fast flowing streams feeding into the River Churnet. Thus, if seeking a weekend in the area, one day could easily be taken up with scenic local walks, one of which passes Dimmingsdale Youth Hostel.

Alton itself has a number of fascinating buildings. Alton Castle was designed by the famous 19th century architect A.W.N. Pugin in a mock Gothic fashion characterised by pointed gables, spires and turrets, the sort of building featured in blood curdling tales of vampires and strange goings-on. This house was in fact built around 1850 virtually on the site of a medieval castle for the then owner of Alton Towers. For some years now it has been occupied by a convent and school. Nearby is Alton Church, dating from earlier times but mainly rebuilt in the last century.

The main attraction for most families is nearby Alton Towers. If the famous Corkscrew rollercoaster or the Grand Canyon rapids are not quite your cup of tea then the Gardens, the Towers, Victorian Talbot Street, or the Nature Trail might be. For we tend to forget that Alton Towers has a magnificent show throughout the entire year. Obviously, the main attraction for the children are the rides, rides and more rides and the main theme park is open from early spring to late autumn. During the late winter, however, the gardens are still open and this provides a good opportunity to visit a dreamland created by the wealth of the later Earls of Shrewsbury.

*continued on page 16*

13

# Route 2

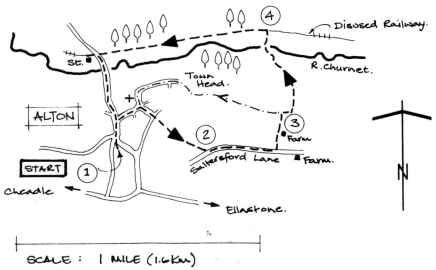

ALTON TOWERS

4

Disused Railway.

St.

R. Churnet.

Town Head.

ALTON

3
Farm

2

START

1

Saltersford Lane

Farm.

Cheadle

Ellastone.

N

SCALE : 1 MILE (1.6 KM)

14

## Route 2

## Alton

START *From the Lock Up in Alton village, just off the B5032 between Cheadle and Ellastone (O.S. Sheet 119 G.R. 074422). There is a limited amount of on-street parking.*

## ROUTE

1. *Walk downhill and turn right into High Street. Opposite the church go right by the cemetery. At the top take the second of the two right turns and then go left through a stile. Continue ahead to the far left corner of the field and cross the stile by the gate. Proceed ahead, once again to a stile, with Staffordshire Way signs, and go left into Saltersford lane.*
2. *At first sight of the farm ahead look for a stile on your left. Go through it and follow the green track up the field to join another lane. (For a short cut, turn left along this pleasant lane back to Town Head. Continue past a traditional dairy farm to the convent school and church, turning left into Castle Hill Road and right into High Street.)*
3. *Turn right, then, once through the gateway turn left and continue down a field and across a stile. After a few steps go left again through a gap and head in the direction of the Towers! You'll see a stile ahead. Cross it and the path winds steeply down a dry gap between tree and rock to a stile below. Go over this, then a track, and cross the footbridge over the Churnet to reach the disused railway.*
4. *At the trackbed go left along the old line until Alton Station, where there are steps up to the main road. Go right and climb back up to Alton village.*

## ACCESS BY BUS

There is a bus service 232 from Hanley to Cheadle, where you change on to Route 238/9. No Sunday service in the winter. There is a daily direct service, X39, from Stoke-on-Trent Railway Station to Alton Towers throughout the season.

15

The walk begins at the Lock Up , and this allows a family discussion on punishment! This honey-comb shaped building was once used by local officers of the law to cool tempers, dry out drunks and keep villains at bay before taking them to gaol. Tempting, isn't it? En route, you might also like to ask why Saltersford Lane has such a name. When in the Churnet Valley it is worthwhile discussing why the old railway and canal to Uttoxeter (remnants to be found on the right of the railway trackbed) followed the line of the river and not the road? Needless to say, everyone will be spotting the rides among the trees at Alton Towers on the other side of the valley.

**Refreshments**

Several places in Alton village.

WALKING ABOVE THE MANIFOLD (Route 9)

# Route 3

**3½ miles**

## Dilhorne

**Outline**  Dilhorne  ~  Newhill  ~  Stansmore  Hall  ~  Dilhorne

**Summary**  This walk follows reasonably well used paths around the traditional village of Dilhorne. It is easy going and crosses a number of fields before reaching Dilhorne Wood and the Foxfield Light Railway. Climbing to Newhill, the route descends gently along a quiet lane and then heads back towards Dilhorne by way of Stansmore Hall and the railway once again.

**Attractions**  The main visitor attraction is the Foxfield Light Railway. Built to serve local pits, this line is still open as a privately-run steam passenger railway which also has a number of freight wagons and locomotives to see. The main terminus is at Coverswell Road near Blythe Bridge.

Dilhorne has for most of its existence been an agricultural area. There was mining in the vicinity of Foxfield but now the slag heaps are gone and the land in most places restored to farming. The church has always been of interest for it has a rare octagonal west tower. A few paces along the road are the Lodges and Archway of the former Dilhorne Hall. The red brick Gothic structure looks totally out of place but the children will probably notice the village playground just beyond, so you will see the gateway from both sides to confirm your judgement!

Nearby, Caverswell is worth a visit. It has a lovely square, a distinctive church and a 17th century castle built on the site of an earlier medieval fortress.

On the route look out for the rich woodland fauna in Dilhorne Wood and the light railway in a clearing, an ideal place to introduce the popular 'Railway Children' novel. Why not make up your own story based on this railway? Stansmore Hall, on the return leg, is a sturdy 17th century stone farmhouse with stone mullioned windows. The electricity pylons introduce a degree of modernity into the latter stage of the walk.

**Refreshments**

Dilhorne has three public houses so is well served for refreshment.

# Route 3

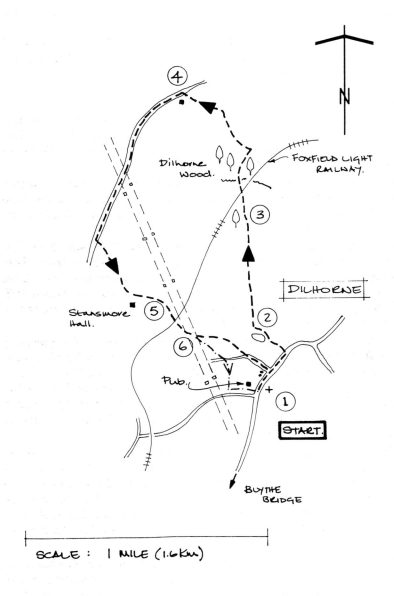

N

④

Dilhorne
Wood.

FOXFIELD LIGHT
RAILWAY.

③

DILHORNE

Stansmore
Hall.

⑤

②

⑥

Pub.

①

START.

BUYTHE
BRIDGE

SCALE : 1 MILE (1.6 Km)

18

# Route 3

## Dilhorne

3½ miles

START  *from Dilhorne Church, on a road which is signed from the A521 from Blythe Bridge to Cheadle (O.S. Sheet 118 G.R. 971434). It is possible to park alongside the road nearby.*

ROUTE

1. *With your back to the church turn right and walk past the old gateway until you reach a turning on the left leading to a car park by the fishing pool. Avoid turnings to the left and cross the stile on the right by the barred gate.*

2. *Walk slightly left across this large field in the direction of the wood and, in the far corner, cross a stile, then pass through a smaller field and another stile before reaching a stile in the field corner leading into Dilhorne Wood.*

3. *Continue straight on, taking care to avoid some of the fallen branches, to the railway line, which is crossed by way of two stiles. Once over keep straight on, to cross a stream before following alongside a wire fence through a wet section to a stile on the left. Cross this and climb uphill, keeping close to the hedge on your right. This eventually leads to a gateway leading on to a track. Go left.*

4. *At the junction with the tarmac lane, go left and follow this, gradually winding down to a point where it widens and the 'No Tipping' signs appear. Look for a stile on the left by a barred gate. Once over, go slightly right across the field and go over another stile and bear left to follow the field's edge to a lane. Keep ahead and pass by the farm buildings of Stansmore Hall. Cross the stile and walk slightly left to meet the remains of an old hedge.*

5. *Follow this downhill towards the electricity pylons and once again cross two stiles guarding the railway. Walk between two marshy areas to cross another stile. Underneath the pylons head slightly left to a stile. Cross this and walk ahead to a gateway which opens on to a farm track, which can get muddy after rain. Follow this gated track by the farm to the road in Dilhorne and turn right by the cottages and continue back to the church.*

6. *There is an alternative route. Beneath the pylons head to the right of the stile towards a barred gate. There is a stile close to this. Cross it and walk a short distance down the lane, but go over a stile on the right. Walk slightly left across the field and prior to the corner there is a hidden stile*

*on the left. Cross this and come out by Charlie Bassets public house. Go left for the church.*

ACCESS BY BUS
There is a regular bus service from Hanley (P.M.T.-X43) to Dilhorne on
 Mons.-Sats. and a Sunday afternoon service 247 calling at the Royal
 Oak in the village.

---

**North Staffordshire Welcome**
 When you are out and about in the area look out for the increasing
number of locally made products available, everything from the
Eccleshall pie to the south of Stoke-on-Trent to Moorlands goat cheese.
The traditional Staffordshire Oatcake, a delicious type of pancake often
with mouthwatering savoury fillings, is sometimes served in local pubs
and tearooms and is well worth a tasting as are the Potteries based Titanic
Brewery ales.
 North Staffordshire people have a reputation for being friendly in a
gentle way and being made welcome makes all the difference. Enjoy your
walking in this lovely part of the world. Spend a little time to get to know
it and you will be richly rewarded as its subtle beauty begins to unfold.
 Welcome to North Staffordshire!

INDUSTRIAL MUSEUM, ETRURIA

20

# Route 4                                              1½ miles

## Etruria

**Outline**   Etruria ~ Etruria Industrial Museum ~ Stoke-on-Trent.

**Summary**   This walk involves a three minute train ride, starting from Stoke-on-Trent to Etruria. Then, the family can enjoy the walk back along the Trent & Mersey Canal near to the recently created Festival Park. The route follows the towpath of the Trent and Mersey Canal back to Stoke-on-Trent Railway Station by way of the Etruria Industrial Museum. It is not a country walk but highlights the importance of canals as green lungs in cities.

**Attractions**   The City of Stoke-on-Trent is the heart of the pottery manufacturing industry in Britain and there are dozens of factory tours and shops open to the public on Mondays to Saturdays throughout the year. Children love to see the design work, the intricate patterns and the hand-painting of fine ceramics. It brings alive the making of household articles such as cups, saucers and plates, as well as more expensive items for the rich and famous. The "Do China in a Day" leaflet lists most of the pottery manufacturers and their opening times, and is an indispensable help.

Festival Park, a new leisure and shopping complex on the old Garden Festival site is a place of excitement for the family with Ten Pin Bowling, an indoor water park, cinemas and a dry ski-slope in addition to shops and restaurants.

On the route, which passes near to the Festival Park, is the Marina and China Garden public house. On the opposite site of the Trent and Mersey Canal are the Sentinel Newspaper offices and the Round House, once part of the Wedgwood works, and now a museum. Permission is required to visit it.

The Trent and Mersey Canal, instigated by Wedgwood, and designed by Brindley in the 1760s was built not only to reduce the cost of transporting china clay from Cornwall by sea but also to link up the entire network from Liverpool to Hull. It is still a mainstream system in terms of leisure traffic and the boats going through the locks provide a source of interest but **do be careful by the water.**

The Etruria Industrial Museum, based on the Etruscan Bone and Flint Mill, is Britain's sole surviving steam powered Potters Mill. Built in 1857 for Jesse Shirley and Son the mill was designed to grind materials for the pottery and agricultural industries and did so up to 1972. Access can

*continued on page 24*

21

## Route 4

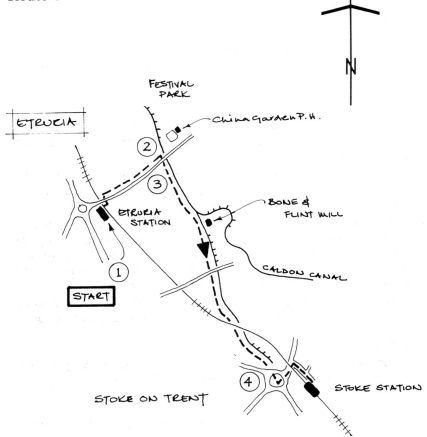

FESTIVAL PARK

ETRURIA

China Garden P.H.

②

③

ETRURIA STATION

BONE & FLINT MILL

CALDON CANAL

①

START

STOKE ON TRENT

④

STOKE STATION

SCALE : 1 MILE (1.6 Km)

N

22

## Route 4

## Etruria

**1½ miles**

START   *At Stoke-on-Trent Railway Station (O.S. 118 G.R. 866469). Travel by rail to Etruria Station. The return journey is on foot, as follows.*

ROUTE

1. *On leaving Etruria Station, turn right and then left under the main Etruria Road. The underpass leads to the other side where you walk ahead to the canal bridge.*

2. *(If visiting the marina, cross the bridge and go left.) Otherwise take the first set of steps down to the towpath and then turn right under the bridge.*

3. *Follow the canal towpath to the junction with the Caldon Canal but do not cross unless visiting the Industrial Museum. Continue along the canalside under the railway bridges and then towards a roundabout which is above the canal system. Go right through the gateway in the metal fencing and to the grassy area in the roundabout.*

4. *Go left here, as signed, to the railway. This brings you out on to Stoke Road. Go underneath the railway and then turn right into Station Road.*

ACCESS

Stoke-on-Trent Station is well served by trains throughout England and by numerous local buses from Newcastle and Hanley.

PIED WAGTAIL   black and white   18cm.

be gained at the junction with the Caldon Canal about half way along the canal section of the ramble. Further along there are two old bottle ovens, where pots would have been fired in earlier decades.

Winton Square at Stoke-on-Trent Railway Station is a lovely setting. The station was the original headquarters of the North Staffordshire Railway and is now partly British Rail and partly the West Midlands Regional Management Centre. The Potteries Centre also occupies one corner and this houses a shop and cafe.

### Refreshments

The China Garden at Etruria. Buffet at Stoke-on-Trent Station. Cafe at the Potteries Centre.

GAP STILE, STANTON

# Stanton

**Outline**   Stanton ~ Softlow Wood ~ Blakelow Lane ~ Stanton.

**Summary**   This delightful and isolated part of the world is on the eastern fringes of the Weaver Hills, not a part which is frequently walked. The Weavers have been quarried extensively in places but this particular ramble crosses quiet farmland. It is gentle for the most part with one or two climbs and wet sections.

**Attractions**   Peace and tranquility! Stanton is a very settled hamlet with a number of fine Peakland buildings nestled around a junction of roads. It was the birthplace of Gilbert Sheldon in 1598 who became Archbishop of Canterbury. His birthplace still exists and the Village Hall commemorates his association with Stanton. Nearby is the village church dating from 1847 standing in a commanding position with extensive views across the Dove Valley.

Nearby is Ellastone, known to Mary Evans or George Eliot, and described with great affection in her novel 'Adam Bede'. Ellastone is thought to be 'Hayslope' in the book and several local buildings have been identified by the descriptions painted in this most readable work. Walking in the area, dubbed "Eliot country", brings to life several of her descriptions of rurality, the 'old world' she describes in contrast to the rapidly changing way of life in towns during the nineteenth century.

On the walk look out for the very traditional stone gap stiles. The shapes ought to be drawn and the numbers counted! There are also two early burial mounds 'Scrip Low' and 'Ober Low' near to the walk but they are not easy to notice. The word 'low' is always confusing because it means high ground rather than lowland!

There are remains of a small mine at Softlow. A cursory glance at the map shows that there are several mentions of the name Thor in this area, presumably a reference to the Thunder God 'Thorr' from our Scandinavian ancestors. Fording the Tinsell Brook on the way back should be good fun.

**Refreshments**
The Duncombe Arms, Ellastone.

# Route 5

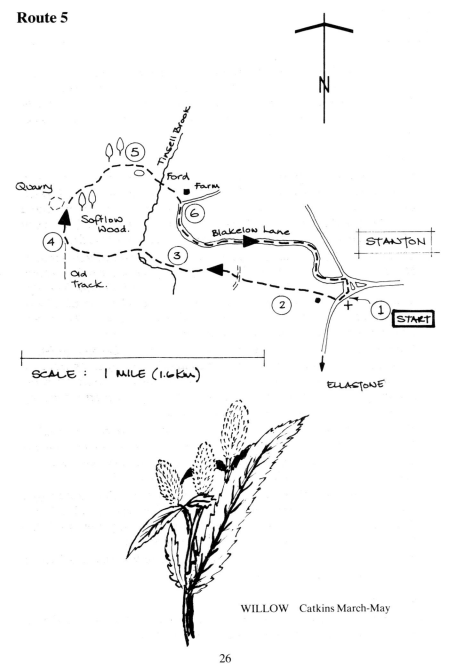

N

Tinsell Brook

⑤

Quarry

Softlow Wood.

Ford

Farm

⑥

④

Old Track.

③

Blakelow Lane

②

STANTON

+

①

START

SCALE : 1 MILE (1.6 Km)

ELLASTONE

WILLOW   Catkins March-May

26

# Route 5

## Stanton

**4 miles**

START *from Stanton Church where there is a limited amount of street parking in the centre of the hamlet but do park considerately (O.S. Sheet 119 G.R. 128462). Stanton is signed from the A52 between Mayfield and Swinscoe - but easy to miss! It can also be reached from the B5032 between Ellastone and Mayfield.*

## ROUTE

1. *Opposite the churchyard there is a gap stile. Go through this and head in a direction to the right of the farmhouse, across gorse covered rough ground. Begin to make your way slightly left to a gap stile between a holly bush and a hawthorn. Cross the stile and head uphill slightly right of the oak tree and towards the top right hand corner of the field.*

2. *Go through this gap stile and then slightly left to go through another. Head slightly right across this field to a gateway, cross the strip field and cross the gap stile on the right to reach the next field. Follow the hedge now on your left down the field to cut through another gap stile. Then proceed ahead until you come upon another gap stile near the corner, which you go through, as you come to a tree-lined brook.*

3. *Walk upstream to a recently created pond and just beyond go left to cross a stile in a boggy area and then go uphill, moving away from the wall on your right as you climb. Go through a gateway and start to curve gently right on a swathe of rich green grass until you meet a track coming in from the left, and with an old quarry ahead.*

4. *Follow the track to the stile by a gateway and, once over, walk slightly right of the track to a stile by the wood's edge. Cross this and walk to the next field corner, covered in scrub and elderberry. Cross the boundary here and then proceed slightly right to cross another stile.*

5. *Continue ahead slightly right, but keeping to the left of the reed fringed pond, over rough land to a tree lined stream which you ford. Walk up a field with a small gully to your right and meet a drystone wall. Go through a gap stile on the right to join Blakelow lane.*

6. *Do not turn left but walk straight ahead and follow this lane back to Stanton, avoiding turns to the left.*

## ACCESS BY BUS

The nearest bus is to Ellastone, two miles from Stanton, with a Mons.- Sats. service between Ashbourne and Uttoxeter.

ROCK OUTCROP NEAR FROGHALL

28

# Froghall and Foxt

**Outline**   Froghall ~ Foxt ~ Moseymoor Wood ~ Froghall.

**Summary**   This splendid walk to Foxt village by way of the old inclined railway and then through Shirley Hollow introduces the walker to an increasingly popular area. Climbing up to the village of Foxt the views of the Weaver Hills and to Alton are delightful. The return section leads into Moseymoor Wood and along well worn paths back to the Caldon Canal and Froghall. An easy to follow walk with a number of climbs.

**Attractions**   Froghall is a fascinating place. As a natural crossing point of the Churnet it was an ideal site for early industrial development and to this day Boltons Copperworks still occupies a large site in the valley bottom. Nearby is the canal and railway and by the former is a picnic site near to the Wharf. This was once an important transhipment centre for an early tramway which brought lime from Cauldon Lowe to be despatched along the canal. The old lime kilns can be seen clearly by the car park.

The canal was designed by James Brindley, a brilliant Derbyshire engineer and millwright and it was while out surveying at Froghall that he caught a chill which within a short time brought about his death. The canal was extended to Froghall by 1776 and then on to Uttoxeter. This latter section was eventually cannibalised by the North Staffordshire Railway.

The Wharf buildings are now a restaurant and in recent years there have been horse drawn narrow boat trips along the Caldon Canal to Consall Forge during the summer.

On the route look out for the old railway trackbed and consider how dangerous it must have been for the workmen and horses on the fairly steep incline. There is an unusual outcrop of rock by Oldridge Farm. How did this get here?

Foxt village is very pleasant with a mainly Victorian church at the top end and the Fox and Goose towards the bottom on the one way road system. Children love the woodland paths through Whieldon and Moseymoor Woods and crossing the Blackbank Brook, a name which reflects early mining in the area. Look out for animal tracks. The latter part of the walk is not a right of way but a concessionary path only so look for the waymarks.

**Refreshments**

Public houses at Froghall and Foxt. The village store at Foxt sells soft drinks.

## Route 6

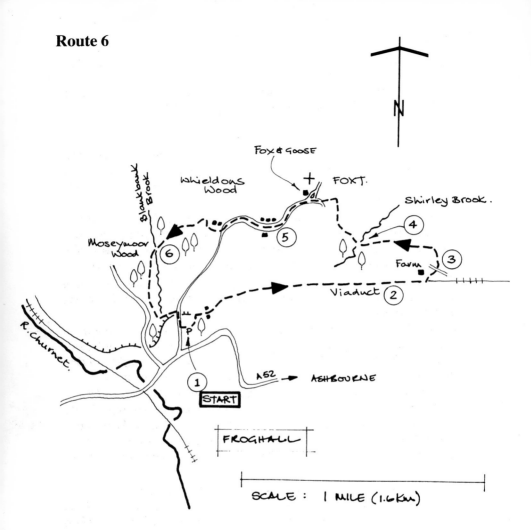

Fox & Goose

Whieldons Wood

Blackbank Brook

† FOXT.

Shirley Brook.

④

Moseymoor Wood

⑤

⑥

Farm

③

Viaduct ②

R. Churnet.

P

① A52 → ASHBOURNE

START

FROGHALL

SCALE : 1 MILE (1.6 Km)

# Route 6

## Froghall and Foxt

**4 miles**

START  *At Froghall Wharf car park, situated just off the A52 between Stoke-on-Trent and Ashbourne (O.S. Sheet 119 G.R. 025475).*

ROUTE

1. *Climb the steps on the left from the car park to a track. Go left and, beyond two houses, take the right woodland path, the old railway incline. This climbs through the woodland steeply, crosses a viaduct and emerges into open country.*

2. *As the incline levels out, look out for a gap stile on the left, the huge rock beyond being the key landmark. Go through the stile, pass by the rock and farm to a gap stile leading on to a tarmac track. Cross this and, after a few steps, go left along the green track to a gap stile by a gateway.*

3. *Once through, follow the field boundary on the left into the valley, and in the next field go slightly right to descend to a track and stile leading into woodland.*

4. *Cross a bridge over a stream with care, then cross the stile on the right to join the track leading upwards to Foxt. The track curves right and comes to a gap stile. Walk along the track to a tarmac road. Go right and then next left. The Fox and Goose is on the right at the road junction.*

5. *Pass by a group of houses and the village store and, after the road bends to the left, look for a path just beyond the cottages on the right by the large concrete pipes. Go through two gateways and follow the path as it curves left to a gateway and then right to the wood. Cross a stile and walk downhill through this wood, right and then left, down steps and to a stream.*

6. *Cross the stream by the stepping stones and climb up to the junction of paths. Go left and in a short while left down steps and across a bridge. Join the narrow towpath and turn left to return to the bridge by the wharf where you go right for the car park.*

## ACCESS BY BUS

Froghall is served by the Leek to Cheadle bus several times a day on Mons.-Sats.

CHURCH AT WATERFALL (Route 9)

# Betley

**Outline**   Betley ~ Wrinehill ~ Betley Mere ~ Betley.

**Summary**   The westernly part of Staffordshire is rich dairy farming country and this easy walk traverses grazing pastures at first. The moss area around Betley Mere is very different though and a walk through a wetter rough commonland and smaller enclosures provides an interesting contrast. Be prepared for softer ground in places and a lush summer growth of plant life beneath the willow flanked man made watercourses which are rich in wildlife. It is rather like a small scale fenland.

    Unfortunately, the mere itself is not accessible to the public but glimpses of the water can be seen throughout the walk.

**Attractions**   Betley village must be, in terms of old buildings, one of the most interesting high streets in North Staffordshire. From the timber framed Betley Old Hall to the early eighteenth century Betley Court there are a fine selection of houses and cottages to be seen, some dating from Elizabethan times. As a settlement it is the 'black and white' timbered houses which make it look so characterful. Betley dates, however, well before the Domesday Book in which it receives a mention. As a token of its importance in medieval times it was granted a market charter in the early part of the thirteenth century. There is, however, no longer a market.

    Betley church is unusual in that it has an extensive surviving timber structure. Most churches in North Staffordshire were rebuilt in stone during earlier centuries unless in a particularly poor area or one endowed with a rich supply of wood. There are several interesting monuments inside devoted mainly to local notables from the Fletchers and Fletcher-Twemlow families.

    En route listen for the trains on the main line from London to Glasgow. You'll be able to see them as you approach Wrinehill and it is good fun counting the number passing in one hour. The reason for the mere's existence is worthy of exploration. Is it man made as are some of the channels around it or is it a glacial scoop-out as with the meres in Cheshire and North Shropshire? The mere and wetlands are good for birdwatching.

**Refreshments**   Several public houses in Betley.

# Route 7

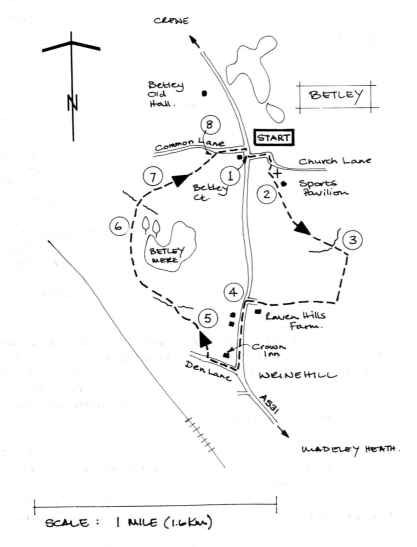

CREWE

Betley
Old
Hall.

BETLEY

⑧

Common Lane

START

Church Lane

⑦

Betley
Ct.

①

✝

②

Sports
Pavilion

⑥

BETLEY
MERE

③

④

Raven Hills
Farm.

⑤

Crown
Inn

Den Lane

WRINEHILL

A531

WADELEY HEATH.

N

SCALE : 1 MILE (1.6 Km)

34

# Route 7

## Betley

**4 miles**

START    *At the Swan public house on the main A531 road from Madeley Heath to Crewe. (O.S. Sheet G.R.118 753486). There is a limited amount of parking in the village.*

ROUTE

1. *Cross the road outside the Swan and turn first left into Church Lane. Follow this around to the right, by the school, then follow the lane which passes the church and leads to the sports pavilion.*

2. *Pass to the left of the cricket pitch and cross the stile beyond the cast iron roller. Keep straight on to the corner of this small field, cross the stile and climb the brow heading left to another stile. Once over, go slightly left across this larger field down to the bulge where you will find steps leading to a sleeper bridge. Cross the stream.*

3. *Climb up this next field, again heading slightly left to the higher of the two oaks and cross the stile just beyond. Go right, and follow the hedge, eventually to cross two stiles into the next field. Within a short distance you will find a stile on the right between a holly and hawthorn. Head down the field to the gap by the larger hawthorns. Keep straight ahead, gently descending to a stile by a gate which leads to a track. Follow this past a farm and cottages down to the main road.*

4. *Go left at the A531 and walk along the pavement for a short way into the adjoining village of Wrinehill, passing by the Hand and Trumpet Inn and the old toll house. Turn right into Den Lane with the Crown Inn soon on your right, and follow this tarmac lane a short distance before crossing a stile on the right. Follow the hedge ahead to a stile, cross it and walk downhill to the field corner, ignoring the first stile on the left.*

5. *Cross the fence beneath the yew and go left along an old track which is now more of a narrow path which can be overgrown in summer. Cross the sleeper bridge over the channel and then go left over two smaller bridges. The path sweeps gently right to a stile leading into a wood.*

6. *Leave the wood by way of a stile and head slightly right to the trees. As they curve right keep ahead to a stile and a bridge. Proceed ahead again to the short looking ladder stile.*

7. *Once over, press on for a short while and then cross the field boundary on your right and go left along the field's edge to another stile. Keep ahead once again and, as the boundary drops to the right, curve gently left to a stile leading into Common Lane.*

8. *Go right to return to the Swan.*

# ACCESS BY BUS
Crosville C84 (Mons. to Sats.) runs hourly between Hanley and Crewe.
The service is operated by Bakers Coaches on Sundays.

THE BLACK LION

36

# Consall Forge

**Outline**    Ipstones ~ Devil's Staircase ~ Consall Forge ~ Ipstones.

**Summary**    The walk begins along a quiet moorland lane with open views but then dips down into Crowgutter. The path skirts the Belmont Estate and descends into rich deciduous woodland eventually plummeting into the Churnet Valley by way of the Devil's Staircase. Passing by one of Staffordshire's remotest pubs, The Black Lion, the path follows the towpath at the edge of the Caldon Canal before climbing once again through woodland and through fields to Ipstones.

**Attractions**    The moorland village of Ipstones sits on high ground; its stone houses nestle together around the village inns and shops. It is in many respects typical of the area in that its once strong agricultural base has weakened and a small industrial estate has been developed to maintain employment. One early writer, discussing the rise of the potato as a crop commented of Ipstones;
'Give a cottager in the Moorlands, with a wife and ten or twelve children, a cow and a rood or two of potato-ground, and you make him a happy man' Not any longer! The farms around are traditional solid stonebuilt buildings from the 17th and 18th centuries and the field patterns, mainly drystone wall enclosures have altered little since those times, a tremendous monument to the wall builders of a previous age.

     About one mile from the village on Ipstones Edge is the Moorlands Farm Park of British Rare Breeds and Domestic Animals Open Farm with over 70 different breeds including Soay sheep, Tamworth pigs, Longhorn cattle and other lovable varieties.

     On the walk, look out for a house which looks like a converted chapel as the Belmont road winds down to the brook. This, in fact, was never a chapel. Evidently, the then local owner of nearby Belmont Hall, fell out with the established church at Ipstones and thus began to build his very own place of worship. Before completion the disagreement was put to rights and so this little chapel was finished off as a house!

     Consall Forge is fascinating. Tucked into this narrow valley is the railway and canal. It looks so tranquil now but it was once, as the name suggests, a hive of industrial activity. The area was certainly used for burning charcoal and smelting iron in earlier centuries. During the 18th century ironstone working became important and brought the canal and the railway, both of which became the property of the North

*continued on page 40*

# Route 8

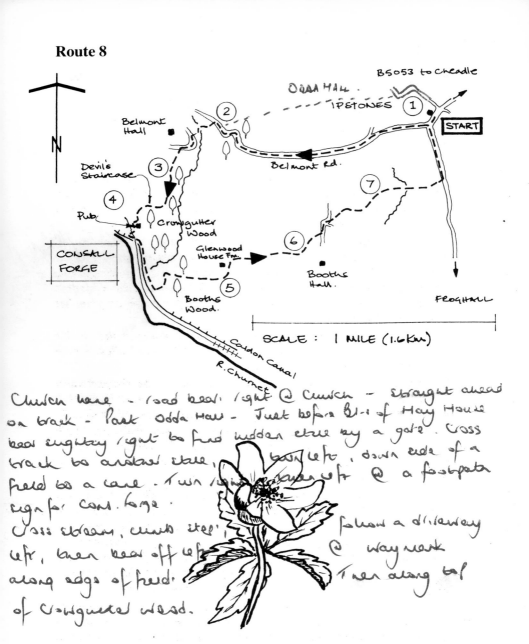

Church lane - road bear right @ church - straight ahead on track - Past Odda Hall - Just before Bt-s of Hay House bear slightly right to find hidden stile by a gate. Cross track to another stile, [?] [?] left, down side of a field to a lane. Turn [?] [?] left @ a footpath sign for Cons. forge.
Cross stream, climb steps left, then bear off left along edge of field.

follow a driveway @ waymark
Then along top of Crowgutter wood.

WOOD ANEMONE   White   April-May

# Route 8

## Consall Forge

**4 miles**

START   *On the main road at Ipstones on the B5053 by Ye Old Red Lion Inn. There is a limited amount of on-street parking in the village. (O.S. Sheet 119 G.R. 021499).*

ROUTE

1. *From the main road, by Ye Old Red Lion Inn, turn right along Belmont Road. In a short while it weaves down between wooded slopes to a quiet stream and, just before a house which looks like a chapel, go left down steps and along a path signed to Consall Forge.*

2. *Cross the old sleeper bridge and pass by an old estate boundary stone. Within a short distance turn right to climb up steps to the lane leading to Belmont Hall. Go left and, as the lane curves right, keep straight on, following the path which keeps company with the woods edge. Cross the stile beneath the horse chestnut and then look for a stile on your left leading into Crowgutter Wood.*

3. *Follow this well worn path to a series of steps, know as the Devil's Staircase, dropping almost literally into the Churnet Valley, which looks more akin to heaven than hell.*

4. *The path comes out at the Black Lion public house. Cross the tracks and go left on to the canal towpath. Pass by the restored Consall Forge Halt and, once under the bridge, scramble up left to a track. Walk directly over this to cross a stile leading into Booth's Wood. It's a clear path ahead climbing ferociously through the wood until it eventually exits at a stile beneath a group of sycamores. Keep straight on across a field, moving gradually to meet the hedge on your left.*

5. *Follow this hedge as it curves gently left to a gate leading to Glenwood House Farm. Walk past the buildings until you come to a junction, with the farmhouse on your left. Go right at this point and follow the track into a field. As this track veers right, continue straight on towards the telegraph pole between trees, then head towards the far corner of the field and Booth's Hall. Before the corner, however, look for an obvious opening on the left and follow this to a stile by a barred gate.*

6. *Head diagonally across this field towards Ipstones village. Once at the track, go left and at the junction enter the field ahead of you. Go slightly left in this small field and then through the gap stile. Turn right and go through another gap stile by the holly and keep slightly left across the field just to the left of the telegraph pole.*

7. *Cut through two gap stiles and then go slightly left again to the field corner where the path cuts down steeply to a lovely stream. Climb up the bank, walk ahead through the field at first but then cut across left to a barred gate and stile. Turn left for the short road section into Ipstones.*

## ACCESS BY BUS

There is a limited Monday to Saturday bus between Leek and Cheadle, calling at Ipstones.

---

Staffordshire Railway in the mid 19th century. The local quarrymen were know as 'The Redmen' because they were usually covered in the distinctive red dust of the ironstone. It could not have been a healthy occupation.

The Black Lion public house was once an old boatmen's inn. It must have been something of a sight when thirty or more boats were moored up along the canal with boatmen and women in colourful dress exchanging a yarn or two about their travels.

A ten minute walk up from the canal leads to the Visitor Centre at Consall Nature Park which was opened in 1989. There are waymarked trails around Pool Meadow and Ladypark Wood allowing access to secluded areas rich in wildlife.

This must be a walk for counting steps. Why was the Devil's Staircase so named? Are there a similar number of steps on the return journey out of the valley? Can you measure the climb in terms of feet or metres?

**Refreshments**

Ye Old Red Lion, Ipstones.

The Black Lion, Consall Forge.

# Route 9

**4 miles**

## Waterhouses and Waterfall

**Outline**   Waterhouses ~ Waterfall ~ Sparrowlee ~ Waterhouses.

**Summary**   The ramble commences across gently rising ground by way of numerous small enclosures to the hamlet of Waterfall. From here it descends to Sparrowlee and it is possible to follow a higher level path back or along the Manifold Track whichever is preferable on the day. The views, once out of sight of the works at Cauldon, are admirable and the walk is one of gentle contrasts. The only real climb is up to Sparrowlee but this can be avoided.

**Attractions**   Cycling is all of the rage in Waterhouses for there are two cycle hire centres and on a good day both empty their stores. The reason is the virtually traffic free Manifold Trail up to Wetton Mill and Hulme End. What a great day this makes with a short walk and an afternoon of cycling and picnics!
   Nearby in Caldon village there is a unique public house, the Yew Tree Inn. The entrance contains polyphons and other fascinating music-making machines which work splendidly.
   Waterfall is one of the loveliest villages in the Staffordshire Moorlands, not in a quaint sense but as a homely group of stone cottages and working farms dotted about the network of lanes, not much altered by the passing decades. The small village green has an old pump and restored stocks but resist the temptation of placing the most truculent member of the family in them. The parish church dates from the twelfth century but with many later additions. It is in a secluded corner on your route.

**Refreshments**   Two public houses in Waterhouses. The Red Lion, Waterfall, usually open weekend lunchtimes.
   Croft Guest House, Waterfall. Light refreshments.
   Lee House Farm, Manifold Trail.
   Yew Tree Inn, Caldon.
   Fish and Chip Shop in Waterhouses.

41

# Route 9

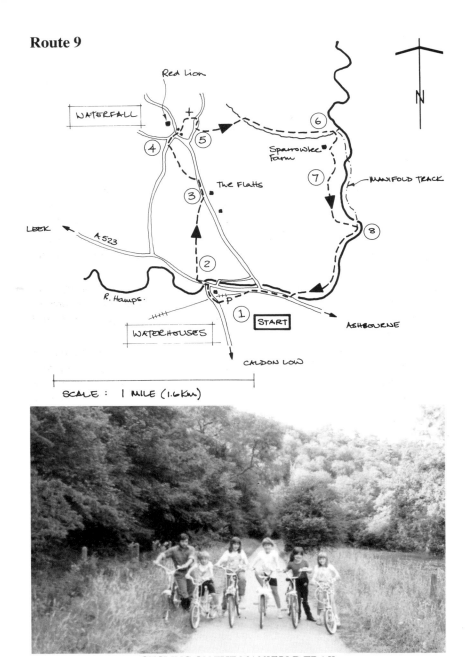

Red Lion

WATERFALL

LEEK

A 523

R. Hamps.

WATERHOUSES

START

P

① ② ③ ④ ⑤ ⑥ ⑦ ⑧

The Flatts

Sparrowlee Farm

MANIFOLD TRACK

ASHBOURNE

CALDON LOW

N

SCALE : 1 MILE (1.6 Km)

CYCLING ON THE MANIFOLD TRAIL

# Route 9

## Waterhouses and Waterfall

**4 miles**

START  *From the car park at the Old Station in Waterhouses, off the main A523 road (O.S. Sheet 119 G.R. 085 502).*

ROUTE

1. *Walk back towards the entrance cutting off right to the road by Ye Old Crown Hotel. Go left and after crossing the bridge go through the gap stile on the right and continue ahead across a field to another gap stile.*
2. *Proceed ahead slightly right and climbing gently through a series of strip enclosures passing through gaps or gap stiles. Enter a larger field with a farm to your right and continue gently up the field to a gap stile leading on to a tarmac lane by The Flatts.*
3. *Turn left and, within a short distance, go left again through a gap stile covered by bushes. Once in the field, head slightly right across another series of narrow enclosures, through a number of gap stiles and eventually to a gap stile leading into a tarmac lane at Waterfall.*
4. *Turn right and continue to a T-junction. Go straight across to the start of a track. Follow this between a cottage, stocks and the village pump to a gap stile. Go through it and across a field to a stile leading to the churchyard. Walk through to the iron gates and on to another tarmac lane. Go right and then soon find a gap stile on the left.*
5. *Once in the field proceed to the next gap stile and then continue downhill, heading gently towards the gully on the right. Cross a stile, a bridge and another stile before turning right to follow the stream down to the Manifold Valley track.*
6. *Just prior to reaching the track go through the gate on the right and follow the signpost indicating your way up the grass track towards Sparrowlee Farm. By the farm go left and this leads to a gateway by another signpost. Follow the track ahead to a gateway.*
7. *Do not go through but keep straight on with the hedge to your right. Walk slightly left to a gap in the far hedge and continue ahead in the next field until you come across a small drystone wall. After this point cut left downhill to a gateway leading on to the Manifold Track.*
8. *Turn right and follow this to the main road at Waterhouses. Turn right and walk back to the Old Station car park. The route is waymarked as for bicycles.*

## ACCESS BY BUS

Waterhouses is served daily by the Shearings 201 bus between Derby and Manchester. There are several other local market day bus services between Leek and Ashbourne.

BUTTER CROSS NEAR CHEDDLETON

# Cheddleton in the Churnet

**Outline**   Cheddleton ~ Deep Hayes Country Park ~ Caldon Canal ~ Cheddleton.

**Summary**   This is an easy walk with one steep bank where care is required. The route takes you over grazing land to Deep Hayes Country Park and then on to the Caldon Canal at Denford returning along the towpath including a section where the canal and river flow virtually parallel.

**Attractions**   Ostlers, Shaffalong and Hollow Lanes, packhorse routes of old, meet in a beautiful part of this large and historic village. Situated here is the ancient church of St. Edward the Confessor, dating from Norman times and with interesting stained glass windows attributed to the famous designer and philosopher, William Morris. Beneath the churchyard on the hillside is the traditional Black Lion public house and nearby are the old stocks, used for decades to calm down those who have been a little naughty. If you enjoy a bit of history and a good yarn the village tour, with one of Cheddleton's own professionally trained Village Guides, is a must.

The two key attractions in the village are the Cheddleton Flint Mill and the North Staffordshire Railway at the Cheddleton Railway Centre. The Flint Mill is most unusual. No doubt, there had been a corn mill of sorts on this site since medieval times but the buildings we see today were developed in the mid eighteenth century most probably by that genius of an engineer, James Brindley.

It comes as a surprise to most visitors that the mill was built to crush flints. The vast majority of such mills were established to grind corn. Flint, however, was well known to pottery manufacturers as an ingredient to whiten their earthenware and Cheddleton Mill was one of a number built precisely for this purpose. The entire process, from unloading the flints from the narrow boat to grinding and settling the resultant slop can be seen at this virtually unique attraction. It is open to the public on weekend afternoons but the exterior can be viewed at any reasonable time. Special care has to be taken with the children as there are many moving parts to discover, several steps to encounter and plenty of water around.

A twenty minute walk along the Caldon Canal, which is very much an attraction in its own right, is the Cheddleton Railway Centre. Of all of the former regional railway companies this one has endeared itself to the

*continued on page 48*

45

# Route 10

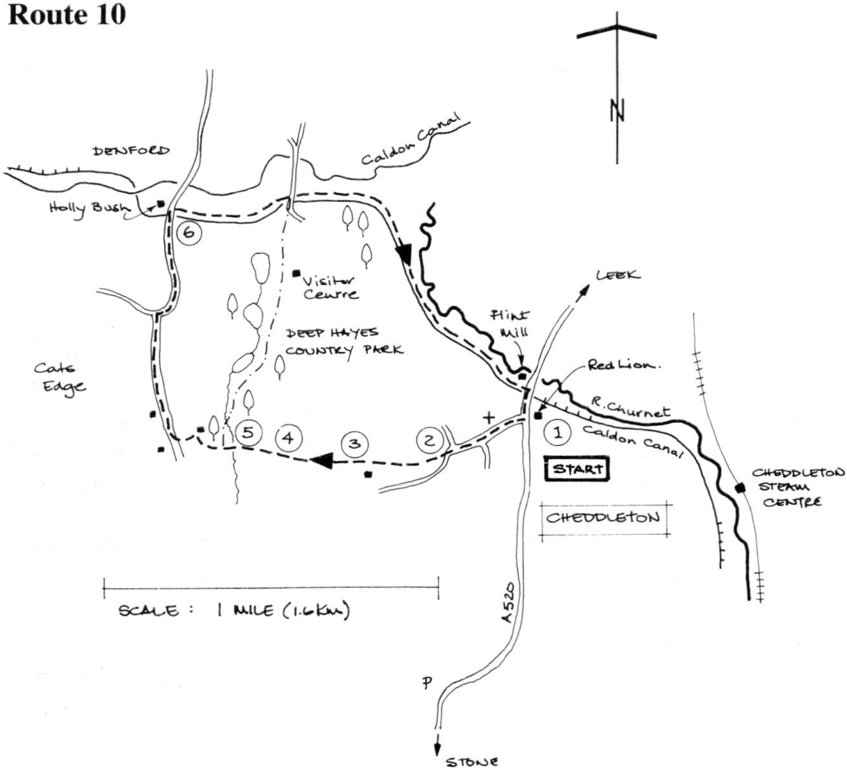

DENFORD

Caldon Canal

Holly Bush

⑥

Visitor Centre

DEEP HAYES
COUNTRY PARK

Cats Edge

⑤ ④ ③ ② ①

LEEK

Flint Mill

Red Lion.

R. Churnet

Caldon Canal

START

CHEDDLETON

CHEDDLETON
STEAM
CENTRE

SCALE : 1 MILE (1.6 Km)

A520

P

STONE

# Route 10

## Cheddleton in the Churnet

6½ miles

START    *At Cheddleton on the A520 between Leek and Stone. There are two lay bys at the top (south) end of the village (O.S. Sheet 118 G.R. 971572). Walk back down the main road to the Red Lion public house.*

ROUTE

1. *Cross the main road by way of the pedestrian crossing and make your way up Hollow Lane, passing the church, the school and community centre. This becomes Shaffalong Lane and, as it turns left, go straight ahead through a stile with a signpost to 'Cats Edge'.*

2. *Walk through a small field to two further stiles then head slightly right uphill. Go through a stile and head slightly right to the farthest point of the line of trees. Cross the stiles here and walk ahead for several paces before crossing another stile on the right.*

3. *Head beyond the telegraph pole to a gate and stile. Follow the track around to the next gate and stile. Once through, go slightly left in the direction of the mounds, where you see a signpost beyond between hawthorn and elder.*

4. *Cross the stile and descend a steep bank with no clear path, through scrub at first then skirting a boggy patch by gateposts (but do not go through them!).*

5. *Go over the footbridge below. (For a short cut through the country park turn right, following the red waymarks along the left bank at first, then along the right bank until you reach the visitor centre and toilet block. Continue ahead along the park access road until the tarmac lane. Go left and rejoin the canal. The concessionary path through the park is sometimes closed mid-winter.)*

   *Otherwise, continue ahead up the bank and then right up to another stile leading into a meadow. Follow the path around the edge of the field to a track and go right. This leads to a cottage and you continue ahead down a green lane to a tarmac lane. Go right, this leads to a bridge over the canal by The Hollybush at Denford.*

6. *Go right on to the canal towpath, then left and follow the canal back to The Flint Mill at Cheddleton. Just beyond, there is an exit on to the main A520 road opposite The Flintlock restaurant. Go right back to your starting point.*

Cheddleton has a daily hourly service from Leek to Hanley (Procters) and an hourly service between Longton and Leek on Mons.-Sats. (P.M.T./Stevensons). Bakers special leisure tour 'Moorland Rider' calls on summer Sundays.

---

hearts of The Potteries. Know affectionately as 'The Knotty', given the company's insignia based on the 'The Staffordshire Knot', the railway is developing as a real visitor attraction after years of hard work.

At Cheddleton Railway Station, a fine building designed by the famous architect cum designer of the last century, Pugin, you'll find a ticket office, small museum, shop and cafe. On most Sunday afternoons in the summer there is also an engine in steam, very often the saddle tank engine 'Josiah Wedgwood' shunting one carriage up and down a siding. The hope is that the company will operate longer distances down the Churnet Valley as soon as it can gain complete ownership of the track.

On the walk itself there are several beautiful views across the Churnet. The canal was built in the late 1770s partly to transport lime and aggregate, coal, flints as well as agricultural goods. Many of the bridges in this area were designed by the famous engineer and architect, John Rennie. At Deep Hayes you will see over the valley the Leek Branch of the canal which is still open to the outskirts of Leek. Count the number of bridges, and look for the marks worn in the stonework by the towropes of the original horsedrawn narrowboats. Deep Hayes Country Park (some locals prefer 'Deep Haye') is based around two pools with a number of waterside trails, picnic tables, a visitor centre and toilets.

**Refreshments**   There are three public houses, a restaurant and several shops in Cheddleton village, and The Hollybush at Denford on the ramble.

# Route 11                              3 miles

## Alstonefield and Milldale

**Outline**   Alstonefield ~ Stanshope ~ Milldale ~ Alstonefield.

**Summary**   This ramble leaves Alstonefield by way of a walled track through fields to a quiet part of Hopedale and climbs an old track up to Stanshope. From here the route reverses back to Milldale where access can be made to the Dove. However, the return route is by way of a steep climb up to Alstonefield village passing by the parish church. The walk involves several strenuous climbs but the views are worth every ounce of energy.

**Attractions**   Standing on high ground between the Dove and Manifold Valleys the village of Alstonefield is a rather captivating place. Its church dates back from 892 but is mainly 14th century and with the former Elizabethan Alstonefield Hall and Georgian rectory nearby, the setting is one of rural charm. In fact, one of Britain's early literary figures, Izaak Walton, known more for his text 'The Compleat Angler' than for his writings about rural England, worshipped in this very church alongside fellow scholar Charles Cotton. The Cotton pew in the church is quite famous.

On route look out for the imposing 17th century stone built Stanshope Hall and in Milldale it is possible to take a rest. If you have not seen it before Dovedale is as beautiful as every text has portrayed. The dream is shattered somewhat when you meet a thousand other folk on the same walk so if you decide to take off along the banks of the delightful Dove choose a quiet moment.

**Refreshment**   The George Inn, by the shady village green in Alstonefield offers good food and drink, and has a family camp site behind it. The Old Post Office Cafe is just around the corner. At Milldale there is a shop and cafe.

# Route 11

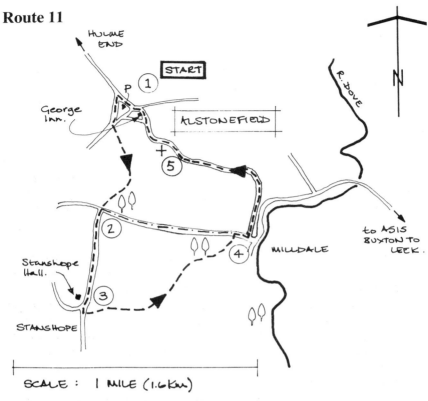

HULME END

START

① P

George Inn.

ALSTONEFIELD

⑤

②

Stanshope Hall.

③

STANSHOPE

④

MILLDALE

R. DOVE

to ASIS BUXTON TO LEEK.

N

SCALE : 1 MILE (1.6 Km)

DRYSTONE WALLS

# Route 11

## Alstonefield and Milldale

**3 miles**

START   *At Alstonefield car park and toilet block. Alstonefield is signed off the B5054 at Hulme End or from the A515 Buxton to Ashbourne road at Newhaven near the Newhaven Hotel. (O.S. Sheet 119 G.R. 131556).*

ROUTE

1. *From the toilet block turn left and left again to pass by the Community Centre on the right and a triangular road junction on the left. Then go left between two stone houses along a walled track. As this veers right go through a gap stile by a gate and keep ahead down a field with the wall on your right, eventually curving right as it narrows to a stile by a gateway.*

2. *The path drops steeply here to a gap stile leading to a tarmac lane. Cross this and follow the rough track uphill to Stanshope. (For a shorter route turn left along the tarmac lane towards Milldale.)*

3. *At Stanshope Hall turn left and left again, signed to Milldale. This rises gently to a summit where you leave the track and follow the path signed to Milldale, following the drystone wall on the left and then keeping straight on through a number of gap stiles until you come to a dry narrow valley. The path descends steeply to the right of a house and on to a tarmac lane. Go right.*

4. *Opposite the Milldale Shop go left and left again by the telephone kiosk. This climbs up steps and a wooded section before crossing a gap stile into a large field. Go left and climb steeply. Half way up begin to walk to your right to a gap stile in the corner.*

5. *Once again, proceed diagonally right across a small enclosure towards Alstonefield Church. Once in the next field follow the path curving right to a track. The track passes by the church and back into Alstonfield through the village green by the George Inn, then left and right to the car park.*

ACCESS BY BUS

Alstonefield enjoys a limited service from Ashbourne and Buxton on Saturdays and from Macclesfield and Buxton on Sundays.

WETTONMILL

# Wettonmill and Butterton

**Outline**    Wettonmill ~ Butterton ~ Hoo Brook ~ Wettonmill.

**Summary**    A steep climb out of Wettonmill unfolds several magnificent views of the Manifold Valley. The route then follows a number of field paths into Butterton before returning downhill virtually all of the way to Wettonmill alongside the sometimes dry Hoo Brook. Wettonmill has become very busy on summer Sunday afternoons although this is not the case on other days. If you wish to avoid the crowds start the walk at Butterton instead as this lovely village is not so busy but do park considerately if travelling by car.

**Attractions**    Wettonmill, no more than a farm and cafe, sitting under the rather brooding Wetton Hill, is a very popular haunt in the Manifold Valley. While not as busy as Dovedale the Manifold Valley is in many respects as beautiful. The one time Leek and Manifold Light Railway passed by Wettonmill and there was a station and passing loop here. What a railway it was. Built at the turn of this century, partly to serve the old mining area but also to stimulate agricultural demand the line was never destined for commercial success. In recent years a small amount of track has been relaid at nearby Hulme End. For a few weeks each June, a miniature steam train is operated and the old station buildings opened up to the public, the proceeds going to charity.

There are a number of caves in the vicinity, the most famous being Thor's cave. Two local archaelogists Thomas Bateman and Samuel Carrington found numerous pots, coins and other artefacts dating from Prehistoric times in or near it. They are now lodged in the Bateman Collection at Sheffield Museum.

The Manifold itself is invariably dry and suggestions as to how the valley was formed and why the river is for most of the year dry as a bone makes for a great discussion on the walk. The river disappears at Wettonmill only to surface through 'boil holes' at Ilam, a good eight miles or so away. Over millions of years the limestone rock has been dissolved by the percolating water and thus the river is flowing underground somewhere. Most theories suggest that the steep sided valleys we see in this part today are indeed collapsed caves of previous underground systems. Earlier in the century one local notable, Sir Thomas Wardle, literally tried to bung up the holes with concrete but nature outbid him. Before long the concrete began to crack!

*continued on page 56*

# Route 12

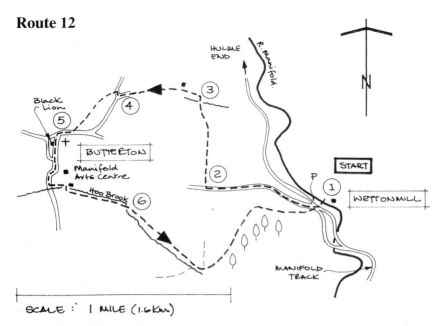

SCALE : I MILE (1.6 Km)

COTTAGE, HOPEDALE

# Route 12

## Wettonmill and Butterton

4½ miles

START   *At Wettonmill in the Manifold Valley (O.S. Sheet 119 G.R. 095561). Wettonmill can be reached from the B5053 via Butterton, or from the B5054 via Hulme End. Alternatively the walk can be started at Butterton Church (O.S. Sheet 119 G.R. 076566).*

ROUTE

1. *From Wettonmill follow the narrow road across the Manifold Trail (which at this point is a minor road) and uphill towards Butterton. After half a mile the road levels out. Look out for a stile on the right.*

2. *Go over this stile, continue ahead to a gate and then a step stile by a farm. Cross another stile and proceed to meet and follow the hedge to a gate. Go slightly down a field to another gate and on to the line of trees in the dip. Cross the stream and go through the gate.*

3. *Climb the bank and when you see a gap stile in the hedge go left across the field to a gap stile to the left of a barn. Cross this and look out for the little gap stile part way up on the left. Go through it, cut the corner of the field and keep in the same direction through small fields towards the telegraph pole where you keep company with the hedge ahead towards Butterton Church spire. Continue to a tarmac lane.*

4. *At the lane go right for a short distance only to turn left through a gap stile and ahead to another by a gate. Cross this and again look for a gap stile on the left. Go through it and immediately through another on your right. Cut across left to a gap stile in the hedge near the farm and then exit from the next field by a stile opposite the church.*

5. *Go right on the tarmac lane by the church and turn left downhill, passing by the Black Lion and the Manifold Arts Centre. As the ford begins turn left towards a cottage. Cross the stream before you reach the cottage. The path curves up to another gap stile and then follows the Hoo Brook into a valley. It eventually joins and crosses the brook by way of stepping stones.*

6. *Continue with the stream now on your right to a meeting of paths where you continue left downstream to rise slightly above the stream bed on to a grassy plain and over a stile into a camping site just before meeting the road at Wettonmill.*

ACCESS BY BUS

There is a Saturdays only service from Leek to Butterton.

55

The spire of Butterton Church, like its neighbour Grindon, can be seen for miles around. The Manifold Arts Centre, once the village school, now displays local arts and crafts, designer knitwear and ceramics.

**Refreshments**   The Black Lion at Butterton provides good food and drink. The Manifold Arts Centre serves refreshments as does the cafe at Wettonmill.

RUDYARD

# Rudyard and Horton

**Outline**   Rudyard ~ Harracles Mill ~ Horton ~ Rudyard.

**Summary**   This easy walk, with one climb into the hamlet of Horton, introduces one of the quietest corners of the Staffordshire Moorlands. Nestled around its thirteenth century church, the hamlet has changed little over the decades. A writer, in 1914, describes the quaint surroundings as 'soothing' the place having an 'undisturbed air'. Seventy six years later, the description is equally applicable for this is part of Staffordshire's old world, a world rarely discovered by the passing visitor.

**Attractions**   Rudyard is marvellous for boating, sailing and other water related activities. It was originally designed by James Brindley to serve as a feeder to the Caldon Canal. In the latter part of the 19th century it became something of a fashionable local resort with the North Staffs. Railway Company bringing thousands from The Potteries to enjoy the surrounding countryside. On one day in 1877 over 20,000 flocked to the lakeside to see the famous swimmer, Captain Webb from Shropshire, swim the entire length. He managed it with great speed! One young couple who enjoyed the area so much that they named their son after it ... Rudyard Kipling, the famous author of the Jungle Book. The Rudyard Lake Railway links the car park and lakeside during the main season and the children love it.

On the walk look out for Harracles Hall, a fine Georgian building and Harracles Mill, once owned by a local notable family, the Wedgwoods. Rising up towards Horton there are several fine views of Morridge Edge and the Peak District.

Horton is full of interest. Your walk takes you into the churchyard, where a cross can be found to commemorate the life and poetry of Moorlands Poet, George Heath, renowned for his sad poems. In many respects his work predicted his own untimely death of a chill at the age of 25. The church, while dating from the thirteenth century, has been restored through the ages including work carried out by the famous Leek architects, the Sugdens, in the last century. It is a splendid country church. The Crown Inn, a fine country pub, stands close by.

Horton Hall is a fine 17th century house of character, which reminded Pevsner, the famous architect and historian, of a Cotswold setting. Nearby is the old vicarage dating from 1753.

*continued on page 60*

57

# Route 13

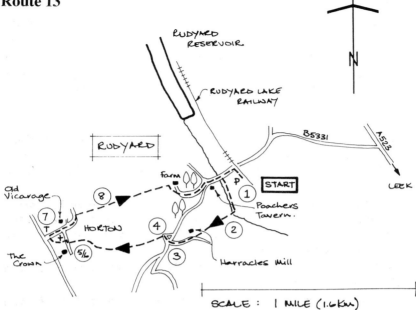

RUDYARD RESERVOIR

RUDYARD LAKE RAILWAY

RUDYARD

B5331

A523

LEEK

Farm

Old Vicarage

⑧

START

P

① Poachers Tavern.

⑦ T

HORTON

④ ②

⑤/₆

③

The Crown

Harracles Mill

SCALE : 1 MILE (1.6 Km)

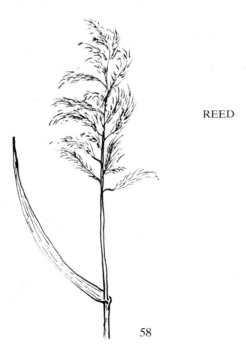

REED

58

# Route 13
## Rudyard and Horton

**3 miles**

START *From the car park situated on the old North Staffs. Railway trackbed off the B5331 between Poolend and Rudyard, signed from the A523 Leek to Macclesfield road (O.S. 118 G.R. 955579).*

ROUTE

1. *Walk back down the access road to the main road, turn left and, after a small bridge, left again on to a path alongside a feeder canal. Follow this until you reach a wooden footbridge in a marshy area rich in reeds and grasses.*

2. *Cross the footbridge and walk ahead, keeping company with the hedge on the right, crossing a stile beneath a tree. You come to Harracles Mill, where part of the feeder and buildings can be seen, as you cross a stile and continue ahead along a track to a tarmac road.*

3. *Walk directly over the road and follow the narrow lane for a short distance to the signed path for Horton on your left.*

4. *Go through two gap stiles immediately, then climb gently up the next field to another stile. Cross the stile and follow the hedge until it drops away to the left. Your path curves right, heading in the direction of Horton Church, to a stile to the right of a dead tree. Once over here, the path slips gently left downhill to a gap in the field corner. Go through, and then turn left to climb up the hill, with a hawthorn hedge to your left, to a small gate opening on to a lane.*

5. *Before you stands a fine country pub, The Crown, should you wish to take a break at this point!*

6. *Step right a few paces, then walk up the steps between a cottage and the churchyard. The path passes beyond the churchyard to a small meadow with an old farm to the left. Your way is slightly right across this enclosure to a telephone kiosk.*

7. *Go right and follow the lane over the brow by the old vicarage, to drop down a tree clad hollow lane. As the road bends left, go through a gap stile on your right by a gate, and walk uphill and slightly right to another stile which you cross.*

8. *Continue straight on across a field to join a wall which you keep to your right. Cross a stile by a stream and keep straight on. As you approach the farm follow the path right to a couple of stone gap stiles which lead on to a track. Go downhill to come out by Rudyard Post Office. Go*

*right and then turn left by The Poacher's Tavern back to the car park. Rudyard Lake is nearby and you might, after all, be tempted to take that little rail ride!*

## ACCESS BY BUS
'Moorland Rider' on summer Sunday to Rudyard or Shearings 201 to Poolend, 1 mile away-daily.

---

A Kipling story book is a must for the picnic if you can keep the team still for long enough. Other activities could include a survey of the grasses and other plants alongside the canal feeder, spotting The Roaches and The Meramid (Inn) as the walk climbs to Horton. A poetry competition stimulated by thoughts of George Heath might work on the return journey.

**Refreshments**   The Crown Inn, Horton.
Hotel Rudyard and The Poachers Tavern at Rudyard.

SHEEP SHEARING

# Route 14                                    **6 miles**

# The Roaches

**Outline**   Tittesworth ~ Upper Hulme ~ The Roaches ~ Frith Bottom ~ Tittesworth.

**Summary**   With The Roaches always in sight the walk follows the road towards Blackshaw Moor for a short while before turning left along an old drovers road to Upper Hulme. It then winds up to Dain Mills and on to The Roaches by way of Wells Farm. The path then descends to Meerbrook through Windygates and by Frith Bottom Farm. There is a short final section along the road to Tittesworth Visitor Centre. There are a number of climbs but none ferociously steep.

**Attractions**   Tittesworth Reservoir has become over the years a place of recreation for locals and visitors alike. Thanks to the development work of Severn Trent Water there is a Visitor Centre at The Lodge and a nature trail around the reservoir. This is particularly good for spotting a variety of birds from the Pintail duck to Greylag geese. There is also a cafe, toilets and a superb children's playground.

Upper Hulme is a village reflecting early industrialisation around the fast flowing brook feeding into Tittesworth. Dains Mill is a good example of a small early waterpowered complex which is unfortunately in ruins.

The Roaches is, of course, by far the greatest attraction on the route. Those unusual weathered shapes will entice the children and so be extra careful here. The family might wish to make a diversion up on to the edge or to climb the well worn path up Hen Cloud. There are impressive views from the tops and it is a real adventure but do keep well clear of the crags so loved by climbers practising for their next expedition.

Meerbrook is a close-knit hamlet, with a Youth Hostel in the old school between the church and The Lazy Trout.

**Refreshments**   The Lodge Cafe, Tittesworth.
The Lazy Trout, Meerbrook.

# Route 14

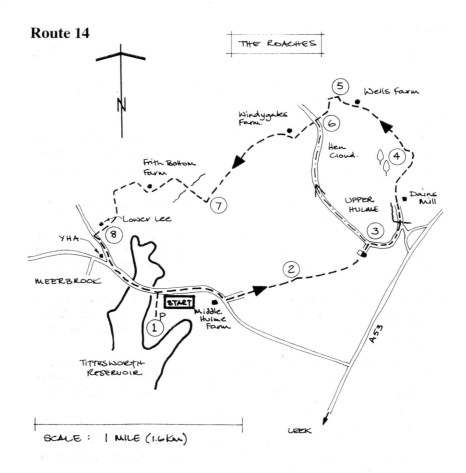

THE ROACHES

N

Wells Farm

5

Windygates Farm

6

Frith Bottom Farm

Hen Cloud

4

7

Daine Mill

Lower Lee

UPPER HULME

YHA

8

3

MEERBROOK

2

START

P

1

Middle Hulme Farm

A53

TITTESWORTH RESERVOIR

LEEK

SCALE : 1 MILE (1.6 Km)

# Route 14

## The Roaches
**6 miles**

START *from the car park at Tittesworth Visitor Centre, a mile off the A53 at Blackshaw Moor between Leek and Buxton (O.S. 118 994605).*

ROUTE

1. *Return to the entrance and turn right. Walk, facing the traffic for a short distance. When the road curves right cross over by Middle Hulme Farm and walk up a track until it bends sharp left. Continue straight on over the stile here.*

2. *Keep ahead to a stile and footbridge leading to the other side of this ancient track. Go right and follow it up to a gateway before a farm. Once through go left up to a stile. Cross this and go right through the farmyard and turn left up to a tarmac road. (For a shorter route, go left here and left again to Windygates Farm below The Roaches - see Number 6.)*

3. *Go right, following the lane around to the ford which you cross, and walk up the track ahead until it becomes a path by the derelict Dains Mill. The path climbs alongside the stream and then bears left to a gap stile by a gateway.*

4. *Join a track, go left immediately, and then keep straight on at the junction and up to Wells Farm. Cross the stile and then your way is signed through the farmyard to a field where you turn right and head for the next stile, with The Roaches beyond.*

5. *Go over this and proceed slightly left across a field to cross another stile. Once over go left along the wall. In a short distance cross the stile on the left and walk towards Hen Cloud but instead of crossing the stile go right down a field to a minor road.*

6. *Cross the road and walk down a field keeping a drystone wall to the right. At the lane go right passing by Windygates Farm. Leave by way of a stile next to a gate and then go left downhill to a stile by a barn. Keep straight on to a gateway and through the next field to a stile by a gateway. Once through, go right.*

7. *Follow the field's edge to meet a small stream and then keep straight on again to a stile in the corner of the field. Choose the second stile and go left so that you are now walking with a hedge on your left as you approach Frith Bottom Farm. Go left through a gateway and then right down to a plank walk on your right. This leads to a track, where you turn left.*

E

8. *Just pass the next boundary hedge go left over a stile. You soon cross another stile, then keep straight on along a well worn path looking for a gateway to the left of Lower Lee Cottage. Walk up the green track to a minor road and go left into Meerbrook. At the junction by Meerbrook Youth Hostel, go left and return to Tittesworth.*

## ACCESS BY BUS

Moorland Rider serves Tittesworth on summer Sundays. P.M.T. X23 serves Blackshaw Moor from The Potteries and Buxton, daily.

RUSHTON SPENCER CHURCH

# Route 15

**2 miles**

## Rushton Spencer

**Outline**   Rushton ~ Rushton Church ~ Staffordshire Way ~ Rushton.

**Summary**   Rushton is a busy crossroads for walkers as it is the meeting place of three long distance walking routes - The Mow Cop Trail, Gritstone Trail and Staffordshire Way. Despite this, comparatively few are tempted on to footpaths to the west of The Staffordshire Way, quiet paths in this north westerly tip of Staffordshire. The route follows the Staffordshire Way for a short section before climbing to the church. It then follows a number of narrow lanes through Rushton Bank before cutting off down to a tributary of the River Dane. The final section is along The Staffordshire Way back into the village.

**Attractions**   Rushton is a sprawling village on the Cheshire border. It is home to the very successful Moorland Goats cheese at nearby Blackwood Hill but this is not always open for passing trade. It also has five public houses so you won't find refreshment a problem.

On the route is Rushton Church. This small and beautiful church has been referred to as 'The Chapel in the Wilderness' as it is well away from the village on a windswept hillside. It would have originally been made of wood but then rebuilt mainly in local gritstone, although much of the internal wood structure remains, as does the restored weatherboarded bell turret. It is not always open but inside it is a very homely church with a number of interesting features.

You'll notice several interesting inscriptions on the gravestones including one to the station-master who served at Rushton for 15 years after the war. Near to the top gate is a sundial and it is worth spending a few minutes practising to tell the time by the sun.

The old Rushton station master's house and platforms, now a private residence, is a strong reminder of the distinctive architecture of the North Staffordshire Railway.

**Refreshments**   There are many public houses in and around the village.

# Route 15

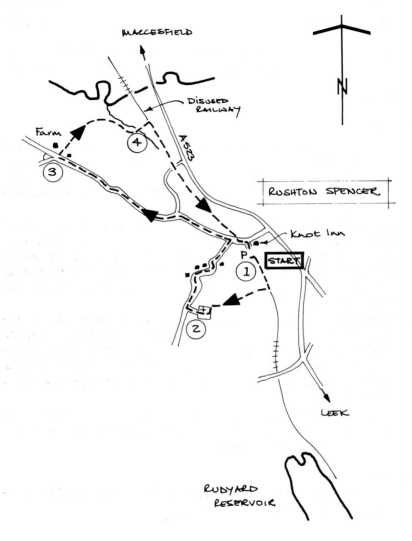

MACCLESFIELD

DISUSED
RAILWAY

A 523

Farm

③

④

RUSHTON SPENCER

Knot Inn

P

START

①

②

LEEK

RUDYARD
RESERVOIR

SCALE : 1 MILE (1.6 Km)

# Route 15

## Rushton Spencer

**2 miles**

START   *At the public car park on the trackbed of the old North Staffs. Railway, the turning on the left after the car park access road to the Knot Inn. (O.S. Sheet 118 G.R. 936625), just off the Leek-Macclesfield road (A523).*

ROUTE

1. *Walk south, away from the Knot Inn, along the old railway until you reach the first bridge. Go underneath, climb up the steps on the left and, once at the top, go left and over the bridge then into a field which leads up to Rushton Spencer Church. Go through the gate, and the path leads up through God's Acre to another gate.*

2. *Continue straight on along a track to a tarmac lane, with views to the left of Rudyard Lake. Go right. The lane curves by houses and drops more steeply, down to a road. Turn left and follow the road uphill for nearly a mile, ignoring a righthand junction. There are superb views to compensate. The road eventually comes to a triangular junction, with a pond in the angle of the junction.*

3. *Turn right here to leave the wood through a small stone gap stile. Go down this field keeping a gully to your left. It is steep sided, so keep the children close to you. This becomes a gentler valley leading to the floodplain of the River Dane. Go right, however, before reaching the Dane, following near to the banks of a tributary until you come to a footbridge.*

4. *Go over this and walk up to the old raised trackbed, passing by the Information Board and up to the old railway. Go right and you'll soon find yourself back by the Knot Inn.*

ACCESS BY BUS

To Rushton Spencer, Station Road Turning. The Shearings 201 Derby to Manchester bus passes several times daily.

INDUSTRIAL MUSEUM, ETRURIA (Route 4)

# Route 16                                    4 miles
## Gradbach and Three Shire Heads

**Outline**    Gradbach ~ Three Shire Heads ~ Hole Edge ~ Gradbach.

**Summary**    The Dane Valley must surely be one of the loveliest valleys in Staffordshire's high country, acting as it does throughout its infant course as a boundary between Cheshire and Staffordshire. The walk involves a steady climb towards Turn Edge along the upper shoulders of the Dane Valley. It then follows an old salt road to Panniers Bridge where the route dips into Cheshire for a while. The return is by way of a rough gated tarmac road along a spring line above the Dane where a number of farms exist. The path then drops down to Gradbach once again.

**Attractions**    Gradbach Youth Hostel, once an old mill, is a favourite for families. Fifteen minutes walk beyond the hostel is Lud's Church, a mysterious fissure shrouded in legend. Children very often come to the conclusion that this was a hiding place for the Luddites, machine breakers fearing for their jobs in early industrial times. A more likely explanation is that this was a secret place of worship for Walter de Ludauk, a follower of the religious reformer John Wycliff, who suffered persecution as a result during the reign of King Richard II. According to Arthurian legend it is also said to have been a fighting ground between Sir Gawain and The Green Knight. It is a damp, cold and secluded place, ideal for letting the imagination run riot!

The village of Flash is about two miles away. This area was once frequented by footpads (highway robbers without horses), and counterfeiters. Hence the term 'flashy', meaning something that looks good but has a hollow core. In fact, the gang of villains began to cause so much trouble along the highways and farmsteads in the area that a crack set of law enforcement officers were despatched from Chester to deal with them. From that time the people of Flash settled down to a more law abiding existence.

On the route the main feature is Panniers Pool at Three Shire Heads. This medieval packhorse bridge situated in such an isolated location says a good deal about the harsh life of the men who led the trains of packhorses bringing salt and other goods across the Peak District from Cheshire. This point, the junction of three counties, in the days when there were three separate county police forces, was also a place where barbarous sports such as cockfighting and animal baiting were carried out. If the police from one county arrived on the scene the gathering would simply escape to an adjoining territory away from jurisdiction!

The views down the Dane and across to Wales are excellent.

# Route 16

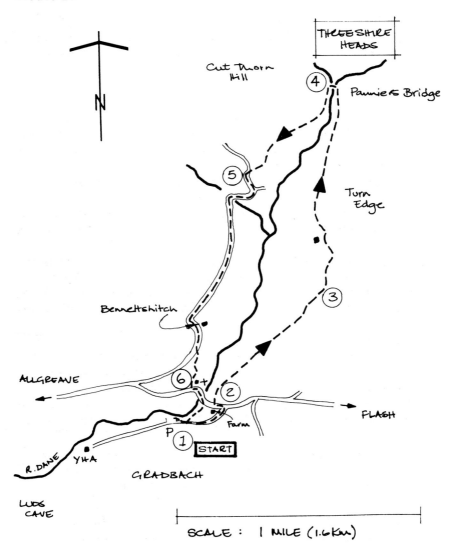

THREE SHIRE HEADS

Cut Thorn Hill

④

Pannier Bridge

Turn Edge

⑤

③

Bennettshitch

ALLGREAVE

⑥

②

FLASH

Farm

P

①

START

R. DANE    YHA

GRADBACH

LUDS CAVE

N

SCALE : 1 MILE (1.6 KM)

# Route 16

## Gradbach and Three Shire Heads          4 miles

START    *At the car park on the access road to Gradbach Youth Hostel, which leads off the link road between the A54 Congleton to Buxton road at Allgreave or from the A53 Leek to Buxton road from Flash. (Car Park O.S. 119 G.R. 998663).*

ROUTE

1. *Follow the waymarked path from the top end of the car park alongside the infant Dane to the tarmac road. Turn left and walk to the road junction beyond the farm. Go left again and as the road drops to a corner turn right through a gateway near the old stone barn.*

2. *Go right over the stone stile by a footpath sign. Then keep company with the drystone wall on your left for several fields as it climbs this gentle ridge offering superb views of the Dane Valley. As the wall turns left walk straight on across rough ground heading for a giant of a ladder stile.*

3. *Cross it, and walk diagonally left across the first enclosure, go through a gateway, then follow the wall round towards a derelict building. Pass to the right of this as you climb to a stile leading to an old drovers track. Go left and follow this up to Panniers Bridge at Three Shire Heads. Cross the bridge and turn left.*

4. *The track curves gently around Cut-Thorn Hill, then, as you begin to see farmhouses beneath, look out for a path through bracken into a wet area and to a stile which you cross. Proceed through a gateway and follow the wall on your left to a gateway leading in to a tarmac lane.*

5. *Turn left and follow this gated lane past a few farms. After Bennetshitch take the signed path on the left and follow it down to a road by a house and chapel.*

6. *Go left and, once over the bridge, turn right over a stile leading into a meadow by the River Dane. Follow the riverside to the footbridge and, once over the mill fleam, go right again to the car park.*

ACCESS BY BUS

The nearest bus, P.M.T. X23 daily, runs along the main Buxton to Leek road stopping at the turn for Flash Village which is a good 2-3 miles away from Gradbach.

---

**Refreshments**    Pubs at Flash and Allgreave.
    Afternoon teas available in Gradbach on the Allgreave road.

FEEDING TIME AT BLACKBROOK FARM

# Appendices

## ROUTES IN ORDER OF DIFFICULTY
**Starting with the easiest:**

Route  4  -  *Etruria - 1½ miles*
Route  1  -  *Barlaston and Wedgwood - 3 miles*
Route 15 -  *Rushton Spencer - 2 miles*
Route  3  -  *Dilhorne - 3 miles*
Route 13 -  *Rudyard - 3 miles*
Route  7  -  *Betley - 4 miles*
Route  2  -  *Alton - 3 miles*
Route  5  -  *Stanton - 4 miles*
Route  9  -  *Waterhouse and Waterfall - 4 miles*
Route  6  -  *Froghall and Foxt - 4 miles*
Route 12 -  *Wettonmill and Butterton - 4½ miles*
Route 11 -  *Alstonefield and Milldale - 3 miles*
Route  8  -  *Consall Forge - 4 miles*
Route 16 -  *Gradbach and Three Shire Heads - 4 miles*
Route 10 -  *Cheddleton in the Churnet - 6 miles*
Route 14 -  *The Roaches - 6 miles*

## PUBLIC TRANSPORT IN NORTH STAFFORDSHIRE
The area covered by this book is well served by public transport in some areas and not so in others. Timetable information, however, is good and for up to the minute information Staffordshire County Council's BUSLINE is very useful. Simply 'phone (0785) 223344 on Mondays to Fridays.

The main operators mentioned in this book are as follows:

British Rail .......................................................... Tel. (0782) 411411
Bakers Coaches ............................................... Tel. (0782) 522101
Potteries Motor Transport (P.M.T.) ......................... Tel. (0782) 747000
Shearings ............................................... Tel. (0942) 44246

Many of the rural services in the Moorlands area of Northe Staffordshire are included in the excellent PEAK DISTRICT public transport timetable published by Derbyshire County Council and is available at the Tourist Information Centres in Ashbourne and Leek. It is also available by post from Derbyshire County Council, Public Transport Unit, County Offices, Matlock, Derbyshire, DE4 3AG. (Current price 40p but please check before writing.)

## TOURIST INFORMATION CENTRES
**Newcastle-under-Lyme,** The Library. Tel. (0782) 618125.
**Stoke-on-Trent,** 1 Glebe Street. Tel. (0782) 411222.
**Hanley,** Potteries Shopping Centre, Hanley. Tel. (0782) 248600.
**Leek,** 1 Market Place. Tel. (0538) 381000.
**Ashbourne,** 13 Market Place. Tel. (0335) 43666.
**Buxton,** The Crescent. Tel. (0298) 25106.

**WET WEATHER ALTERNATIVES** Completely or partly under cover. Check opening times by 'phone before travelling.

**Alton Towers,** Alton. Tel. (0538) 702200; Europe's premier leisure park.
**Blackbrook Farm Animal World,** Winkhill. Tel. (0538) 308293.
Rare breeds and Shetland Centre.
**Brindley Mill and Museum,** Macclesfield Rd., Leek. Restored water powered corn mill built by James Brindley (1752). Tel. Leek Town Information Centre.
**Chatterley Whitfield Mining Museum** Tunstall. Tel. (0782) 813337.
Story of Coal Mining.

**Cheddleton Flint Mill,** Cheddleton. Tel. Leek T.I.C.
Flint Mill with twin waterwheels.
**City Museum and Art Gallery,** Hanley. Tel. (0782) 202173.
Displays of Art, Costume, Nature, Ceramics, etc.
**Etruria Industrial Museum.** Tel. (0782) 287557.
Steam Powered Potters Mill.
**Falconry Guest House Otter and Wildlife Sanctuary.** Tel. (0538) 754784.
Tours available but by appointment only.
**Festival Park,** Hanley. Tel. (0782) 263611.
Leisure and shopping facilities on Garden Festival site.
**Ford Green Hall,** Smallthorne. Tel. (0782) 202173.
16th century timber framed farmhouse.
**Foxfield Light Railway,** Blythe Bridge. Tel. (0782) 314532) (weekdays) 396210
(weekends).
**Gladstone Pottery Museum,** Longton. Tel. (0782) 319232.
Museum of British Pottery Industry.
**Manifold Arts and Craft Centre,** Butterton. Tel. (05388) 320.
Designer knitwear, local arts and crafts, exhibitions.
**Moorlands Farm Park,** Ipstones Edge. Tel. (0538) 266479.
Over 70 different breeds of animals.
**Newfields Gallery,** Foxt. Tel. (0538) 266334.
**Newcastle Borough Museum and Art Gallery.** Tel. (0782) 619705.
Houses one of the largest and most complete collections of Borough charters.
**Private Museum of Prams,** Dilhorne. Tel. (0782) 396301.
Unique collection - By appointment only.
**Staffordshire Peak Arts Centre,** Cauldon Lowe. Tel. (0538) 308431.
Crafts and local exhibitions.
**The Natural Sciences Centre,** Newchapel. Tel. (07816) 5205.
Conservation, alternative energy, astronomy, etc.

## POTTERY MANUFACTURERS and OTHER INDUSTRIAL TOURS
**There are dozens of pottery manufacturers offering factory tours and welcoming visitors to
their museums and shops. Please ask for the 'Do China in a Day' leaflet which
comprehensively lists them.**
Available from Tourist Information Centres.

## CYCLE HIRE
**Brown End Farm,** Waterhouses. Tel. (0538) 308313.
**Peak National Park Cycle Hire Centres.** Tel. (0538) 308609.
**Cycle Hire Centres** at Waterhouses, Ashbourne and Parsley Hay near Hartington.

## COUNTRY PARKS AND NATURE TRAILS
Those listed are in the countryside. There are also a number of parks within the city of
Stoke-on-Trent.
**Castern Wood Nature Reserve,** near to Wetton village in the Manifold Valley.
**Coombes Valley Nature Reserve** off the A523 (1 mile walk from Bus 201).
**Consall Nature Park,** near to Wetley Rocks off the A52 (No Bus).
**Deep Hayes Country Park,** just off the A53 at Denford (Regular Bus 218).
**Greenway Country Park,** signed from the A527 to Biddulph (Regular Bus 6 to Brindley
Fold and 1 mile walk).
**Hanchurch Hills,** south of the A519 (No Bus).
**Hawksmoor Reserve,** near Cheadle on the B5417. (Limited Bus service from Cheadle).
**Ilam,** walks in National Trust grounds of Ilam Hall. Signed from A515 north of
Ashbourne. (Limited bus service from Ashbourne and Buxton).
**Park Hall,** off the A520 road. (Regular 106 Bus).

**USEFUL READING**
  **Heaton P.** Staffordshire. Shire County Guide.
  **Lumsdon L.** Staffordshire Walks. Simply superb.
  **Palliser D.** The Staffordshire Landscape.
  **Staffordshire County Council.** Staffordshire and the Peak. Offical Guide.
  **Staffordshire Federation of Women's Institutes.** The Staffordshire Village Book.

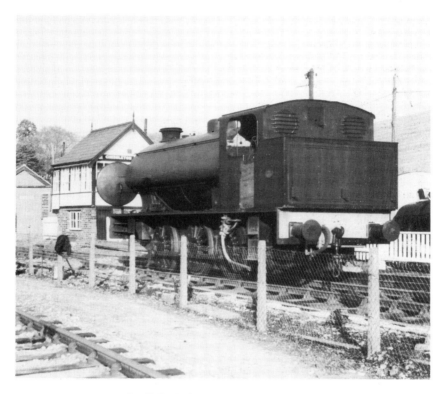

RAILWAY CENTRE, CHEDDLETON

BUTTERTON

CHEDDLETON FLINT MILL

STATUE OF JOSIAH WEDGWOOD IN WINTON SQUARE, STOKE-ON-TRENT
Josiah Wedgwood (1730-1795) was the son of a small master potter. With a "fortune" of £20 inherited from his father he built up the family business, opening the famous Etruria Works in 1769. Here he produced cheap but well-designed tableware for ordinary families as well as expensive items such as jasper ware for the luxury market. Much of his output was exported to colonies and to Europe, where one of his customers was Catherine the Great, Empress of Russia. To obtain supplies of china clay from Cornwall and to transport his pottery safely for export he took a leading part in the building of the Trent and Mersey canal. He ranks alongside men such as Richard Arkwright and James Watt as one of the pioneers of the eighteenth century Industrial Revolution.

# FAMILY WALKS SERIES

**All titles at £3.25**

**Family Walks in the White Peak.** Norman Taylor. ISBN 0 907758 09 6.
"the best Peak District short walks guide yet published." — the Great Outdoors.

**Family Walks in the Dark Peak.** Norman Taylor. ISBN 0 907758 16 9.
Companion to the first title.

**Family Walks in the Cotswolds.** Gordon Ottewell. ISBN 0 907758 15 0.

**Family Walks around Bristol, Bath and the Mendips.** Nigel Vile. ISBN 0 907758 19 3.

**Family Walks in Hereford and Worcester.** Gordon Ottewell. ISBN 0 907758 20 7.

**Family Walks in the Downs and Vales of Wiltshire.** Nigel Vile. ISBN 0 907758 21 5.

**Family Walks in South Yorkshire.** Norman Taylor. ISBN 0 907758 25 8.

**Family Walks in the Wye Valley.** Heather and Jon Hurley. ISBN 0 907758 26 6.

**Family Walks in Mid-Wales.** Laurence Main. ISBN 0 907758 27 4.

**Family Walks in South Shropshire and the Welsh Borders.** Marian Newton.
ISBN 0 907758 30 4.

**Family Walks in the Staffordshire Peak and Potteries.** Les Lumsdon. ISBN 0 907758 34 7.

**Family Walks in Cheshire.** Chris Buckland. ISBN 0 907758 29 0.

**Family Walks in South Gloucestershire.** Gordon Ottewell. ISBN 0 907758 33 9.

**Family Walks in Snowdonia.** Laurence Main. ISBN 0 907758 32 0.


**Ready Spring 1991**

**Family Walks in North West Kent**
**Family Walks in Berkshire and North Hampshire**
**Family Walks the Teme Valley**
**Family Walks in Sedgemoor, Avalon and Mendip**
**Family Walks in Oxfordshire**

Other titles in preparation.


*The Publishers, D. J. Mitchell and E. G. Power, welcome suggestions for further titles in this series; and will be pleased to consider other manuscripts of regional interest from new or established authors.*